Journey Of The Mad

JULIE STACEY

DEDICATION

My grandmother, Pauline Johnson, who is amazingly still in my life, but sadly claimed by Alzheimer's cruel hands. By word of mouth she was a popular clairvoyant and opened my mind to the great mysteries of the universe.

AND

My sons, Phil Stacey, Lewis Stacey and Jake Ridgewell and my beautiful granddaughters Jessica Jane Stacey and Ruby-Joan Shepard-Stacey. My life would be empty without them.

AND

My amazing daughter in laws, Charlotte Ridgewell and Tyler Liesa McDermott-Shepherd, who have given me so much love and understanding. They are like daughters to me and I feel blessed they have come into my life.

AND

My beautiful aunt, Gail Crofts, who despite enduring
the most terrible loss, continues to smile and remain strong for her family. I really do admire her strength and she is a second mother to me.

AND

Chantel Crofts, who shone light into this world with her smile and generosity, but sadly left the earth plane far too early

AND

My mum, Jane Collins, who still guides me through life from the spirit world. Her voice is always right.

I love you all with all my heart

CONTENTS

Green Cat Books

www.green-cat.co/books

ACKNOWLEDGEMENTS

My deepest gratitude to one of my best friends, mentor and fellow author, David Rollins. David started writing poetry whilst in a mental health unit, and now spends his time writing a range of books. He also supports numerous people with various disabilities, whilst managing chronic illnesses himself. He truly is an inspiration to me and without his support, this book would never have been published.

My brother and sister-in-law Sean and Alison Stacey who helped me keep my family together, of which I will be eternally grateful.

My childhood was also brightened by Lisa Matthews, my aunt, sister and best friend. We were born nine weeks apart and she has always been a great source of laughter and a shining light in my life.

A big thank you to my closest friend, Clint Quinn. He has only ever shown me kindness, support and unconditional love. He is such an unique person and I am so grateful to have such a fantastic friend.

I would also like to thank my work colleagues, Esther Cameron, Gretta Tharratt, Annette Mendy, Laylaa Chander, Fiona Doherty and Girish Bhavsar. They have cheered me on and shown so much understanding, kindness and support. Without them, I would have given up on employment and plunged into a very dark place. I will never forget that.

A massive thanks to my CPN, Steve Hebbron, an amazing and a valuable member of the NHS Mental Health Team. His visits help me through and gives me perspective when my thoughts are bleak. Keep up the good work Steve.

Lisa Greener at Green Cat Books for accepting my work which has given me a chance to follow my dream of becoming an author.

INTRODUCTION

Twenty years ago, I was taken from my home by the police and placed in a cell for the night. I don't remember if I slept at all, but I do remember singing and dancing around. I was euphoric and having an adventure. Life was a game to be played and I felt liberated and free.

The next morning, I was taken to a room where I was seen by a doctor. When she told me I had Manic Depression, it meant nothing to me. I was basking in my new-found confidence and energy. I felt very special and believed I was famous. Not long after I was taken to a mental health unit and sectioned.

Manic Depression now known as Bipolar Disorder, is a serious mental health condition which is recognised by extreme mood swings from high to low and vice versa. I have bipolar type 1, where during a high phase of the cycle, mania develops and psychosis sets in.

The highs bring such a tremendous sense of confidence and self-assurance. I feel so energised and powerful. Anything is possible and I am out to achieve my dreams.

However, the glory never last long. Mania creeps in like a slippery snake and insight is lost along with most inhibitions. Behavior can become very reckless and false beliefs grow as psychosis begins to play its game. On many occasions I believed I was being followed along

~~with having~~ cameras rigged up in my home. I found this very frightening.but exhilarating too.

Highly excitable, thoughts race, continually changing from one idea to another. Speech becomes so rapid, trying to converse has left me feeling breathless. Sleep is scarce as the mind never quietens down. I have had periods of being awake for 48 hours. You can imagine how exhausting it is.

Anger and irritability are big culprits during a high. It's so overwhelming I ~~have literally felt as if steam~~ was ~~coming out from the top of my head. It really~~ is painful. ⓘ
In the past, I was often verbally abusive towards others, when manic. It's common for people with this disorder to become aggressive and abusive towards others, which creates a great deal of upset. Mental illness can be very lonely.

It is agonising when you come down from a manic phase. Not only are you enveloped in a crushing depression, there are consequences to be faced. People have lost partners, family members, friends, jobs and even their homes due to their behavior and bad choices. It tips your life upside down.

My depressions have lasted months, where I have slipped into a state of total misery, with excruciating anxiety. There are no words to express how dark it is in that space. It is torture! The only relief to be had is through sleep.

and out bursts of

Yet there is a magical side to this illness. As well as being destructive, the energy from mania can be very creative. I wrote these poems during a manic phase of the bipolar cycle. They were literally flowing through my mind, continually, leaving me with no choice but to get them down on paper. It really seemed like the poetry was creating itself, coming through me not from me. Not having a great interest in poetry, I was surprised at this phenomenon. It was a very profound experience which I believe prevented me from being hospitalised and sectioned. Even more surprising, I didn't sink back down into a crushing low, following the manic state. For the first time in twenty-one years, I felt okay. I was even able to face work without being overwhelmed by dread and fear. A miracle? Yes definitely. I have since made some positive changes in my life and I am moving forward and feel renewed.

From my manic state, I introduce to you my journey through some of my highs and lows. These include reflections on some of my psychic and spiritual experiences and thoughts on life and love.

The lack of punctuation throughout part one, reflects the continuous flow of thought during mania, that is both energising and exhausting.

Part two, is a section of haiku, which is a Japanese form of poetry, consisting of three lines. The top and bottom having five syllables and the middle seven.

Coming from mania, the poems are raw and give insight and understanding into the daily struggles and challenges of living with a mental illness. From my heart, I welcome you to "Journey Of The Mad".

Part 1

Through My Highs and Lows Spirit Held My Hand

1. My Sons

If I could give my sons
just one gift,
it would be inner peace.
But hindsight is not that kind
and as I look back
I see a person so vacant
and I can only assume
she will catch up

2. Chantel

I saw your face,
Was it grace I smiled
Those flowers
pushed through so urgently
Our connection brief
The only words spoken
danced within minds
"These are for my mum," you said
from world to world

3. Brett

He came through the wall and disappeared through the
ceiling,
my three-year-old self repeated.

Trick questions could not take away my truth
as she grasped for hers
of the boy of the shining light , *raiching peace*
Her brother I described .

4. Locked In

Locked in mind
Bound by chains
In fear
High voltage walls
Dry desert beyond
No escape today

5. Mum

You closed your eyes Blondie
when I wasn't looking
Slipped into your dream
I was fully aware though
when you came and hugged me
in mine

We will meet again
that I do know
as you reach out to me
Spontaneous connections
through space time

I miss your chatter Mum
and making your tea
One flat sugar
Half a teaspoon of milk

6. Bombs

Do you know
how it feels to scream
Blood flying
Family dying
I pray
you never do
as you judge the victims
of those leaders wars

What did you say
The benefit claims
and all jobs taken
First on the list to be housed
I hope they are
They deserve a rest
with losses endured
and hearts torn
whilst you eat chocolate cake
and stare at mobile screens

7. Media Lies

Love
will show you more
than media lies
that locks you up
Prisoner of fear
Hostage to anger
and ready for the kill
Unaware of the big planned cull

8. Dulled

Today I am an Olanzapine zombie
Dreams dulled
Nightmares gather round
Doubts are in plenty
My head is a weight
but hopefully the sun will shine tomorrow

9. Hospital Again

I once told a doctor
to take that fucking look off his face
after I told him I talk to dead people
and their advice is quite good
So up yours Mr Quack
Then he came at me
with locked doors
and a dose of Clozapine

Muscle spasms it hurts
body and mind
I talk to you
from a tunnel
as my head drops
The weight of just being
Still they pump their drugs
and my mind is dulled
But I can still hear the calling of my soul
and I want to go home
Then I find out lithium too
No consent given
but got to get to the loo
Dizzy sick walk

over the moving floor
so I crush the lithium
Swap these I demand
plus the other no more

Young woman next to me
a child really at eighteen years of age
A headbanger of walls
and slasher of arms
She strangles her own neck
The sheets have a use
in her continuous battle
with obsession
to meet the call of death
My heart it raced
that night the ambulance was called
I lay there
Hard to breath
Please young lady
please don't die

There's a traveller in here too
her beauty faded by a demon
Yet her eyes still glisten
as she runs through the muddy garden
No shoes
asking for a cig

The crying lady is wailing again
heard all through the ward
her regret running deep
Her family turned backs
their disappointment
for the god she let down

And the one who begs the nurses to kill her
so frail and weak
she really does make me weep
And anxious Anne so kind
she tries to help her eat

Miss Nervous is in a state
an insult flicked in her face
She couldn't handle her anger
Smashed her head so fucking hard
against that stone wall
Only then
would she play snooker with me

The bitchy cold nurse
daring to tell the patients
there'll be no days spent in bed
She won't be ruling me
that I am sure
So I tell her to fuck off out the door
I won
but I really need to get out of here

10. The Message

A simple carrier bag carried the message
not the books it held
all those years ago
when it showed
Alice in Wonderland
and the wisdom of the Queen
discussing the miracle of believe
Great advice
More like a prediction really

as it happened
my first miracle

11. Still Waters

Still waters of the mind
brings forth sweetness of a kind
unknown before
this enchanting peace
of wells so deep
But until that time
you will fretfully sleep

12. The Strangest Trip

I rowed a boat with demons
observing
as they rode pure waters
a gift from above
And my heart ached
they looked so familiar
as if we had met
in another life

Hell wasn't too bad actually
nor wading through vomit
the sin of greed
And the houses
Windows showing anger and hatred
does not rid evil
Why contribute to pain

13. Zombies

Lunatics
twat waffling all the way
of victories dreamt
Greed and power
Pockets built of gore
Whilst we watch the tv
not hearing our call
And the children play
whilst zombies stand small
bombed bloodied and poor
And destiny cries out
stand tall please stand tall
But that's ignored
as the poor blame the poor

14. Spirit

Spirit is no resident of the skies
as most ignore
this intelligence of nature
residing within us all
Life sweet eternal
in its heavenly form
The universe bore the earth
as birthed we were
from the mystery
of this planet

And what is time
A large chain
made up by man
Makes us forget

Its only movement and flow
Forces in creation
of all that is
And we have no time
only all the time
in eternity

The universe moves with such direction
carrying us forward
destination unknown
in this space time
weeping
so very sad
as it carries its creation
that is threatened with destruction
at its own children's hands

15. Awe

Awe
This is new
and in one moment
I knew
being alive
as the flow
takes my breath
And the sky
a beautiful and changing picture
forever hanging above
that most fail to see

I can run through mountains
chains broken and freedom re-claimed
But coincidences rush at me so very fast

and shit
now I've turned mad

16. Mania

I like my mania
It gives me confidence
and more
Manic panic attacks
frightening beyond belief
Exhilarating
adrenaline rush with
racing thoughts and heart
stuck in déjà vu
Present moment
one second ahead
So terrifying
and enjoyable
that most found weird
Will always be grateful to madness
for giving me insight and tools

17. Mercury

89.87 days it takes mercury
to fly around the sun
What would happen if it exploded
this mass of burning fire
Could it send its shooting stars to earth
in 23 days
or a year
burning us in hell in its feverish fire
Or would it just die out
at the perishing of the universe

18. A Ghostly Following

I spoke to a ghost
It showed me
flowers music and get-well cards
following me
like a puppy
wanting a home

19. Synchronicity

Living life in the moment
where land becomes clear
Synchronicity flowing
with a future paved out
to all that we have
Evolutions whispers
for our destiny
to be more than
hatred and pain

20. Madness

People think I am mad you know
but that is okay
truth laid bare
at both ends of my story
In the light
realities
that maybe, you need to see
And the darkness
no veil there

21. Misery

The mind they tell
is a canvas of life
Just need to get out this head
where misery lies
and my imprisoned soul
locked in with demons
a head full of hell

22. Northern Lights

We had plans
Northern Lights
and simple ones
like Christmas
until madness arrived
Same old story

You made me feel real
those few months shared
I really did miss you
and your enchanting lilt
Regret cut deep
after you stepped out
and closed the door

23. A Gift

Down through the tunnel of time
past met present
And she asked me
what is it you fear
Look at me

my youth in the hands of Nazi bastards
and still I dance with my mind
to remain free
And from Auschwitz
she gave me the gift of humble
a companion I will keep until I die

24. Insanity

True
when you're insane
it's others that are mad
We pay into their system
and never step forward to break their fucking rules
And on we go
pushing a trolley full of shit
as they lead us down a stairwell
to their well thought out hell

25. Esther

My friend Esther
helped me find my feet at work
Took a year of sweat and struggle
until she came along
all strength and mysterious power
I will never forget working
side by side with Esther

26. Come Home

Whispers
with their subtle ways
asking

why are you missing this ecstasy
where the sea holds the sky so gently
and the clouds with their happy silent chatter whilst
holding hands
Imagination has no walls
as it rolls on into infinity
holding our souls so possessively
weeping and laughing
"awaken and come home"
it asks

27. Divination

Why is it that
he who pulls the tarot
holds the card
to freedom and choices

Questions in quantities
Answers of quality
But sadly blinded
they try and pull
the strings of the divine
and on they go
shuffling those cards

28. My Reality

My reality merges with yours
in a sea with depths of
music forests and stars
with flying galaxies
I feel so bold
with the possibilities

of growth of mind
Can I share it with you?
Happy Tuesday
I clap my hands
and do an airplane dance
across Braunstone Park

29. Universal Mind

Inner worlds of forces
blends of battle grounds
Murderous fires
and songs so sweet
vibrating high these strings of joy
It's all a hall of mirrors
Jung's Universal Mind
Actualities brought forth
to somewhere we match
Those endless sunny days
or those of bitter cold

30. Hugged By An Angel

When I was hugged by an angel
in my angry plight
and teary mind
no joy was brought
as she whispered in my ear
just sobs of despair
at what she had to tell
fine tuned
"It is in your hands my dear
you must help yourself"

31. Stabbing Backs

As choices go
I played my hand
and they adore me
Though some
they hate me
with their minds spewing cruel
Stepped stones become slippery
as I find my way home
but at least
on top of this mountain
the breeze heals

And as I move towards my light
you can go to hell
If you think your words can mess with my mind
and take me into your murky world
I can see through you
a compensation of madness
My sadness runs deep
at your own rough plight
and the person you could be

32. Dance With Me

Do you dance inside
as I waltz with you inside my mind
Let me lead you to a world of magical stars
as I see the wanting in your eyes
that match that of my soul

33. Spot On The Floor

Staring just staring

at a spot on the floor
failing to push open
a mind too heavy
with a dry thirsty brain
Between sleeps in plenty
feel smashed to bits
The hammer so relentless
I yield to its blows

34. Creation

An explosion
burning gases abound
Astounding reaction of life force
from particle so precise does it blow
One instant of no end
that our minds cannot know
This voyage of endless
billions of years just go
in a lightning and slow crawl
from one eternal blast
that we call existence
is the essence of now
But they grab fight and grumble
and shout out that is mine

35. New Reality

How in such happiness
a sadness spills out
of those blinkered by hatred
sketching their death riddled fate
I see humankind's funeral will be the most joyful
with a magnificent magical wake

No sorrow drenched grief from nature
as it basks in the richness
of this long overdue date

36. Observation

As it was
the sea did swap over
But there were no rocks at the bottom
Just sinking sand
with an allowance of breath
and observation
of the waving plants and nosey fish
Much to be learnt
as I wait for the lift

37. Hope
Stars become dulled
as eyes grow reluctant by these thoughts
My dust-filled life
and future
All unbearably grim
Yet never leaving my side
the glimmer of a loyal hope

38. A Good Day

Today has been a good day
But the thing is I sent a text
to sing a song
She thinks I'm mad
but that's okay
She believes in Jesus anyway
And as all gods go for a walk

they laugh and talk in a carefree way
Minds will soon be at peace
but our choice that will be
in death or life
it's all the same
just a different claim on fate
But these leaders they try to make us think
we must be a certain way
as they punch each other's minds
They drink champagne and pinch our wine
A gleeful wait
On fascism they shall dine

39. The Asylum

What's it like in the Asylum
I feel safe from myself
but it gets boring
And sad
as I watch minds that have been messed with smashed
out of their heads
The smell of anxiety hangs with an uncurable
hopelessness
And there is a unique social madness
All is hard to forget
But maybe there is a dream
and in time
a miracle occurrence
Heads will no longer hurt

41. Madness Sweet

The wind blew hard
I was dealt a card

of madness sweet
as god pointed at me
sights of glory
My frustration is tough
but so is life
and unattainable love
I will be back
and no strive will I cause
As Jesus lived
a spiritual man
As too was Lennon
shot in the head
by man mad
It's them
wanting the truth to be dead
And as they rule
no peace they give
And I'm sat on a park
as the rain falls around
The mud smells sweet
but no flowers grow
And fate will come
then man will know
that peace on earth
won't be a show

42. Christmas Blues

Well summer's over
Christmas will be next
Last year's was shite
Borderline hell
meets an overdose
of anxiety plight

I try and reach out
but it comes to no good
Scraps of the mind
that throw out unkind
But I know there is much more
than the hurt shouted out
that clouds the love
of mother and son

43. Within That Madness

Random question
do you like your mania
I replied
"within that madness
my soul was touched
as the stone it never belonged to me
the lesson and my downfall
before the gateway to dawn
showed me power
within all's control"

44. To High

Too high
Losing track
Memory poor
What day is it
Where's my key
and lighter
It's all going wrong
So angry
I could smash my flat

45 Before I Die

Dandelion whispers
to capture our soul
Make a wish
before I die
Please it pleads
hear the trees cry
Help the world
before it dies

46. John

My friend John
Gone
in a joint death
of a cloud of fumes
Oh John
where did you go
My one true friend
throughout first time madness
you kept me safe

47. Stand Your Ground

When my mother said to me
"stand your ground"
I was shocked
She is dead you see
However
firmly
she pushes me on
into these hills
wild and green

48. Happy Depressive

Happy depressive says Mr Campbell
I can relate to that
Happy sad it was
when a decision was made
She drives me mad
What else can one do
but to walk away
from this destruction of self
The path is not easy
Its demands do not change
that in order to heal
is to feel the pain

49. Those With Homes

My God it's so cold
as I sit alone
BHS after hours
And I wonder
why eyes look so dead
of those with homes

50. Innocence Soul

Little spider
innocent soul
They will kill you
Stamp
or a newspaper whack
Minding your own business
while their fearing minds
forget all life sacred

Creation of the universe
Atoms you are
So run little spider
run and hide

51. Mixed Mood State

High low high
Mixed state mood
Which way will it go
There's no internet connection
I sit up all night
chain smoking and drinking coffee
Waiting for the crash
or the next flight

52. Hidden Sky

You are missing today
dearest hidden Sky
by clouds dulled
And the leaves from your watered trees
whisper a sacred song
whilst I sit on this bench
and allow the sounds to refresh me
No fighting of thought
No sinking
Just being

53. Whilst I Weep

Loss of inhibitions
does make me a fool

JULIE STACEY

I feel so flat
why is life this cruel

And once again
I face the crowd
A head held high
and a mind that cries

Whilst I weep
It's like they see weak
This feeling is heavy
Just can't grasp hold

Discarded on the floor
A beer can
Reflection of me
Crushed
Feeling like trash

Who owned you?
Alcoholic
or youth
heading that way

54. Where Do We Go

Where do our thoughts go
when we die
Thinking
Feeling
Do they simply
fade into no existence
And we become
just a thought in broken hearts

55. Followed

They're following me you know
and watching secretly
The good and the bad
Equal visitors
to my TV and phone
They have bugged my home
I think I must be Jesus
And as I sink down
I realise
My shadow and my light

56. The Most Simple

Once mind stilled
magic takes hold
An unexplainable experience
of beauty coming forward
Colours of meadows, seas and mountains
No going back
Only visits of learning
to fathom
the most simple

57. Boring Normal

No high
but with grace no low
Just boring normal
until you came through
A medal you gave to me
and kind words that held me up
"you're a winner" you said

I don't know why
but thanks Mum

Part 2

Haiku Poems into Darkness and Light

1
A mad woman me.
No hospital bed needed.
Please, just let me write.

2
It's all gone quiet.
The darkness is descending.
Just have to wait now.

3
In my misery,
they are so much more than me
and I think of death.

4
Clumsy is my name.
A mind cluttered with dark thoughts.
An odd person me.

5
What a mad woman!
She threatens to smash my head,
and scares me today.

6
It buries my soul,
then lifts it up to heaven,
I have gained knowledge.

7
The star is spot on
as it guides me through this life.
It gives me comfort.

8
She touches my soul.
I just don't understand life.
Glad they do not know.

9
No routine today
as I fly high with the stars.
They all applaud me.

10
Another love lost.
Getting used to it again,
in my misery.

11
Wow how fantastic!
My life could not be better.
Secrets shown so clear.

12
They call me stupid,
yet I know much more than them.
They are the blind ones.

13
Oh life is so clear.
Is this a beautiful dream?
Glorious I see.

14
Mundane is clever,
if you get into the flow
life fits together.

15
Up at the ceiling,
I look down at my body.
Strange, but very nice.

16
Jess is coming round.
Love my granddaughter to bits.
We sit and do art.

17
Unrequited love.
Can't wait to see her again.
It's enough for me.

18
The advice was good.
She came to me in a dream.
Years after her death.

19
Is it just boredom
or depression creeping in?
Can't handle much more.

20
Medication now.
I accept it and take it.
Side effects are bad.

21
Just cannot sleep now,
as my mind goes on and on.
Highs can get you down.

22
What are they thinking
as I come back down to earth.
Shit, what have I done.

23
I was so happy.
Then he left when I got ill.
I look back sometimes.

24
I miss my high state,
when I come back down to earth.
Life is just a bore.

25
Back at work today.
Oh my god some things have changed.
Overwhelmed again.

26
What are they thinking,
as I walk among the crowd?
God, this is no joke.

27
I want to die now.
This hell on earth is crushing,
but I love my sons.

28
I do not care much
as I smoke away my life.
Just nothing to do.

29
What is it I want
In this terrible dark life?
Wish I was clever.

30
Frustration hits hard.
Such a useless person me.
Life feels so heavy.

31
It's so bad today,
can't even get out of bed.
Why can't I be well?

32
Not hungry today.
It is hell trying to swallow.
Scared of losing weight.

33
The day seems so hard.
My God how do I do this?
Good for nothing me!

34
What are they thinking?
Am I good enough for them
as I try and work?

35
Going to the gym;
I feel a bit happier.
Can this be the way?

36
My mum died today.
Never thought this would happen
in my manic state.

37
What am I today?
Feel like a fucking zombie!
Death feels attractive.

38
I look at the door.
It's so cold out there today.
My mind just feels dead.

39
Wow, it's beautiful
as I gaze into the sky.
The depression has lifted.

40
Yes, magic at last
as my highs show me much more.
I understand now.

41
In the flow today
just sitting here and writing.
This is new to me.

42
Nice to feel normal
as I gaze into the stars.
Hope I don't go high.

43
"What's the time?" I ask
"Time to heal" Angel replied.
Good, so fed up now.

ABOUT THE AUTHOR

For as long back as she can remember, Julie has suffered with depression and anxiety. In her late twenties, following the death of two close family members, eighteen months apart, Julie experienced her first episode of mania. Shortly after, she was diagnosed with Bipolar Affective Disorder and has since been hospitalised several times.

She has worked as an Employability Tutor for seven years and is currently working part time at a local college in an admin role. She also writes in her spare time and aspires to help others get more from their life's, by eventually producing books in the field of mind, body and spirit.

Other Authors With Green Cat Books

Lisa J Rivers –

Why I have So Many Cats

Winding Down

Searching

Luna Felis –

Life Well Lived

Gabriel Eziorobo –

Words Of My Mouth

The Brain Behind Freelance Writing

Mike Herring –

Nature Boy

Glyn Roberts & David Smith –

Prince Porrig And The Calamitous Carbuncle

Peach Berry –

A Bag Of Souls

Michelle DuVal -

The Coach

Sean Gaughan –

And God For His Own

Elijah Barns –

The Witch and Jet Splinters:

     Book 1. A Bustle In The Hedgerow

    Book 2. The Shadow Cutters

David Rollins –

Haiku From The Asylum

Horsey

Monster In The Fridge

Brian N Sigauke –

The Power Of Collectivity

Bridgette Hamilton –

The Break The Crave System…7 Steps to Effortless Lifelong Weight Loss

Michael Keene –

For The Love Of Tom

The Other Life

Richard Tyndall –

The Aldwark Tales

Steve P Lee –

Oblivion Trilogy:

Oblivion

The Department 44 Files

Assault On Charlestown

Truth C Matters –

I Rest My Case

Deborah Carnelley –

Milo

Dinky The Mermaid

Tianna

Zapher Iqbal –

Lucy At The Snake Sanctuary

Jon Carvell –

Chaos In Camelot

Amber Purnell –

The Plug Monster

Daddy, Daddy, What's That Sound?

Shirley Cawte –

Fine Wine From Chipped Cups

Jennifer L Rothwell –

The Firelighters:

   Book 1. A Spark Of Fire

Danny Hainey –

The Adventures Of Maddie And Liv

Betty Valentine –

A Twist Of Starlight

James McCann –

Fairy Unfairly

Timea Ashraf –

Bibi And The Butterfly King

Diana Hardy –

A Dog Is For Life

The Adventures Of Molly And Angus

Victoria McDonald –

Billy's Red Ball Saves Christmas

Betty Long Legs

Laura Billingham –

A Time For Grace

12 Impey
∠E3 3³SW

ARE YOU A WRITER?

We are looking for writers to send in their manuscripts.

If you would like to submit your work, please send a small sample to

books@green-cat.co

Green Cat Books

www.green-cat.co

42228156R00033

Printed in Poland
by Amazon Fulfillment
Poland Sp. z o.o., Wrocław